About the Authors

Neighbours, friends, bandmates, playwrights, and now poets, Spencer FitzGerald and Peter MacDonald have been creating together ever since they figured out they could. Over the past fifteen years the two have found a home in creating music: writing and performing music with east coast alt pop band "With Violet" and having composed the book and score for nationally touring musical "Trummp the Musical" in 2019. Music has always been something that they crave, but addiction is a lifelong journey, and they're excited to have taken the plunge into poetry.

Addictions Anonymous

**Spencer Crawford FitzGerald and
P. A. MacDonald**

Addictions Anonymous –
Whatever Your Fix May Be

Olympia Publishers
London

www.olympiapublishers.com
OLYMPIA PAPERBACK EDITION

Copyright © Spencer Crawford FitzGerald and P. A. MacDonald 2022

The right of Spencer Crawford FitzGerald and P. A. MacDonald to be identified as authors of
this work has been asserted in accordance with sections 77 and 78 of the Copyright, Designs and Patents Act 1988.

All Rights Reserved

No reproduction, copy or transmission of this publication
may be made without written permission.
No paragraph of this publication may be reproduced,
copied or transmitted save with the written permission of the
publisher, or in accordance with the provisions
of the Copyright Act 1956 (as amended).
Any person who commits any unauthorised act in relation to
this publication may be liable to criminal
prosecution and civil claims for damage.

A CIP catalogue record for this title is
available from the British Library.

ISBN: 978-1-78830-237-1

First Published in 2022

Olympia Publishers
Tallis House
2 Tallis Street
London
EC4Y 0AB
Printed in Great Britain

Dedication

This book is dedicated to our pushers Alex FitzGerald and Noel MacDonald. Without them, none of this would have happened.

Acknowledgements

Thanks to our family for fuelling our addictions since '97.

We are beyond grateful to our parents, Sean, Lynn, Ronalda, and Peter. Thanks for all you've given us both. We've come a long way and have you to thank for the view.

Thank you to our partners, Sarah Newell and Laura Westcott, respectively. Your patience, passion, love, and enthusiasm are what drives us to create and continue creating.

We would like to acknowledge the artistic talent and continued support of Victoria FitzGerald. Thank you, Vick, for lending your hand and enhancing our work with your vision.

We would like to express appreciation to Kristina Smith, and the entire editorial and production team at Olympia Publishers for their dedication and long hours spent on this book. Thanks for taking a chance on us and for making our dream a reality.

Lastly, to the reader. We would like to thank everyone who picks up this book and takes the time to read it. In a world of clicks and likes, this is truly an indescribable feeling. What is a writer without a reader anyways?

D. R. U. G.
Daily. Recreationally. Used. Goods.

A blank page,
Such a sudden rush.
The following is filled
With love and with trust.

Please, step inside,
Shoes are fine.
Don't judge us by our cover,
There's none at the door.
Our substance is in our pages
In hopes you do adore.

Sit, make yourself at home.
Welcome to our mind.
We'll take you,
Poem by poem.

A drug may mean something else to you
Than what it means to us.

Daily. Recreationally. Used. Goods.

Introducing our addictions.

Sincerely,
Spence & Pete

AFFECTION

Tattoos

This infectious feeling
Sends me in a spiral.
My heart you are stealin',
Love for you has gone viral.

Smile like a candle,
Lights up the room,
Leaving marks like a vandal,
Sweet like perfume.

Your love's left a mark on me,
Black ink and a story.
Places only we can see
Marking territory.

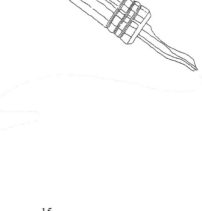

Six Little Letters

Girlfriend addict gets name tattooed,
And claims he will not regret it.
Girlfriend addict turns into ex-girlfriend addict,
Now those
Six little letters etched into his skin
Cause him nothing but pain,
Asking the same old question:

Who is Olivia?

The Levee

Controlled by emotion,
Heart on my sleeve,
A slave to devotion,
I promise you'll see.

Staring in the distance,
Blue eyes staring back,
I knew in that instance,
I was under attack.

If it is human nature
To fall like I did,
Does a pine make a sound
In the forest amid all the madness,
Stood a girl without glasses.
Blue eyes like the sky,
And bright like the sun.
I knew in a moment, she was the one.

For, it was not physically I was under attack,
But me and my emotions, we haven't looked back.

If an iPhone Gave Life Advice

You see, I look for an outlet;
Charge, recharge, repeat.
You should look for in a person,
What an outlet gives to me.

It fills me with a juice of life,
A love I can't describe.
With every touch there comes a spark, just for
Him and I.

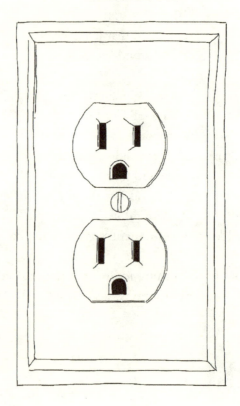

Fight Night (The Main Event)

In the blue corner weighing in at 195 pounds
Is a man who simply will not just lie down.

In the red corner, a foe we know too well, with a
Knockout total
Of X to the nth. Regardless of sex, and a face like hell...

The man takes a few punches at the ringing of the bell.
He throws,
He misses,
He stumbles,
He fell...

Knees are weak,
As he leans against the ropes.
The crowd whispers,
The lights come on.
It seems as though all hope
Is gone...

But he counters with a jab, a quick 1-2.
This fight isn't over, it is far from through,
Supportive hands on his shoulders,
There's always round two.

The man steps back into the ring;
A bit weary, bit worn,
Determined to win,
He will not be ignored.

He was born to win this fight,
Losing is not in his DNA.
With an uppercut, a left hook,
A mean mugged look, this summer born
Defeated, the whole world is shook.
The man has won today,
The crowd does go wild.
His corner looks on, hoping
No rematch for a while.

The fall means nothing yet;
The rise means all.

For all the fighters who have lost the fight;
You will be remembered, you've gone with grace.
Every time the bell rings, and the gloves are
Laced.

A big fuck you to cancer,
A big love you to all.

NARCOTICS

Cuppa Day

Caffeine Stains
On my shirt,
They say, 'Oh so much,'
Gets rid of morning hurt.
Becoming such a crutch.
Upon me and in my mind,
It's what I think about.
Moments after welcoming day in, and showing night out;
I don't feel alive until
That mixture hits my mouth.

The caffeine stains on my shirt
Are never coming out.

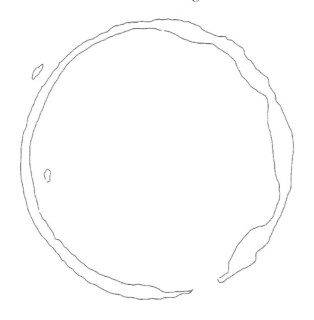

Lake Thought

Totally high and off the cuff. Needs to be refined.
Please pick away.

One Too Many

Life's a long day,
Bathing in your glass.
Turn the right way,
The wrong way fast.

Peering at the bottom,
I can't believe my eyes,
Tricks, they must be playing.
"Nar"

Stone Coloured Glasses

I need her
Like the sun needs the sky;
A drug, you're my high.
And,
I feen for her
Like a cigarette in
The hand of a white guy.

CONNECTIVITY

Texting Untitled

You think because
You are my friend on Facebook or online.

You can feel all my reacts. Into my life you spy.

You can see a smile on my face, as I am strolling by.
But if I yelled
out in
the rain,
there'd
be
no
friend
in
sight.

Sitting behind a ten-inch screen is where most feel alive.
Lightning rods and plastic
to keep
their batteries high.

Will someone
Please
Explain
To me
Just how we've arrived—

In a time where likes and clicks
Is worth more than what lies
Before human eyes.

Words

Words;
Impressions on the wall.
Pictures scream a thousand moments;
Yet one word says it all.

Help.

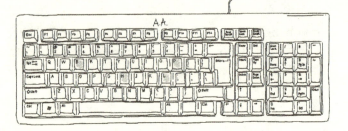

Can I Hear That in a Sentence Please?

When looking for perfection,
Don't go looking at complexion
on a screen.
But looking for social media's 'perfect'... social media
isn't always what it seems.

Who defines perfect?
Point it out to me on a page - would you prefer a screen?
It is only when you can't that you'll
Know what I mean.
It's what's on the inside that
Counts and that matters,
And until you agree.
You'll be climbing that
L
A
D
D
E
R
To the top of the peak, where the oxygen's weak.
Where you look for perfection;
When it's love you should seek.

Can I hear that in a sentence?
Love's a life sentence, so look for connection,
Instead of perfection.

FEARS

Knock Knock

'Knock Knock'

I sit in silence.

'Knock Knock'

Praying no one knows, I am here.

'Knock Knock'

I don't want any violence,
Nor blood shedding tears.

'Knock Knock'

The noise getting louder,
Now the pressure is on.

'silence'…
just for an instance…
The pressure is gone.

I hear a car engine
Roaring away,

Meaning I'm safe
For another day;

If you haven't yet discovered,
I hid.

For, this is the work
Of an introverted kid.

So knock on my door,
Perhaps there's a chance here.

It's a cat and mouse game,
A suburban won't answer.

Thanatophobia

Just let me live, afraid to die.
Wonder why we are born to die.
Dry your eyes for better or for worse.
We are born to die.
Please don't cry.
This is the human curse.

A Hat

A hat covers my head
Like makeup to a face.
A band-aid, a trick mirror.
Platform shoes on a short guy.

We have so much to show.
(yet choose to hide.)
Beauty lies beneath the skin that I
Long to touch,
Ache to hold.

Good Boy

You might disagree.

But being remembered as just a 'good boy' doesn't sound
That 'good' to me.

Here it is, a second controversial call.

I would even argue it's better not to be remembered at all.

GAMBLING

Swing Away

Funny. Tomorrow isn't promised.
I'm healthy,
Happy,
Relatively good weight.
Funny. Tomorrow isn't promised,
As I await my fate.

Shocking really! Tomorrow isn't promised.
I've made plans.
Got class,
Have girls to kiss.
Shocking really! Tomorrow isn't promised.
No matter how many promises I inflict.

Tragedy. Tomorrow isn't promised.
I tried,
Pushed,
Forgot to say goodnight.
Tragedy. Tomorrow isn't promised.
Gambled — Lost to LIFE.

Craps

Standard die has six sides.
1, 2, 3, 4, 5, 6.
I take the roll,
Let life have her pick.

Beyond the Physical

Be tomorrow, be what it may.
For it can't be much sadder
Than a day like today.

Losing a legend, a brother,
A friend.
No wasting time, no belief in an end.

Beyond the physical, the river runs deep.
To remind the physicals, what it all really means.

Be tomorrow. Be what it may.
Surviving this shit, thankful each day.

Thin Line

Walking life on a thin line,
Thinking 'bout the day,
She's gonna take mine.

CONSUMERISM

The Things The Things

'The things, the things I buy for her.'
Therefore, she'll love me more.'

'The things, the things he buys for me.
To me, they mean nothing.'

It's up To You

Spending hours spent working to the bone;
Just to buy some plastic, a tablet or a phone.
It doesn't make much sense, but I guess it's up to you.
How would you spend your hours spent
Fancy living? In a shoe?

Kids

Money is not important to me.
We live the way we live.
Money starts to seem important to me,
At the thought of having kids.

Daily Interactions

[Enter Pin.]
'Good morning, Tim.'
Withdraw Cash?
[Confirm.]
Request Denied.

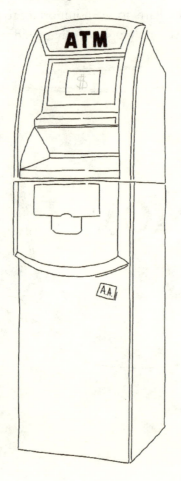

Tagalongs

How do we get to Heaven?
How do we get to Hell?
Do we knock on the door?
Do we ring the bell?
'I don't want what you're selling'
A loud voice yelled,
Though, I'm not selling anything.
I'm just looking for
Heaven
Or
Hell.

Flowers on the Windowsill

Flowers for sale,
Death is the cost.
Each pedal sold, is one soul squashed.

While you move through this grieving phase,
Why not purchase a nicer vase?

Flowers for sale,
Death is the cost.
Give up your wallet, for a life that is lost.

CPSIA information can be obtained
at www.ICGtesting.com
Printed in the USA
LVHW031824070722
722894LV00003B/91